SHARE JESUS WITHOUT FEAR

A Prayer Journal

SHARE JESUS WITHOUT FEAR

A Prayer Journal

WILLIAM FAY

BROADMAN
&HOLMAN
PUBLISHERS

NASHVILLE, TENNESSEE

SHARE JESUS WITHOUT FEAR
PRAYER JOURNAL

Copyright ©2005 by William Fay
All Rights Reserved
10-digit ISBN: 0-8054-4065-8
13-digit ISBN: 978-0-8054-4065-2

Broadman and Holman Publishers
Nashville, Tennessee • broadmanholman.com

Dewey Decimal Classification: 269.2
Evangelistic Work \ Witnessing

Printed in the United States of America

YOU CAN DO THIS!

This journal has 160 pages in it. And long before you reach the last one, you'll already be sharing Jesus "without fear." I promise you.

It's not because there's some magic formula inside. It's not because you're going to be learning a lot of things you don't already know, probably. But there's just too much prayer that's going to be happening between now and the end of this book for you to fail at this. There's *no way!*

In fact, *no one* fails when they're telling others about Christ. No one!

Have you ever felt like a failure as a Christian before? Have you ever gotten put out with yourself for not being more generous, more compassionate, more disciplined, more grateful, more accepting of others? It's not hard for us to get down on ourselves, because we do come up short in so many areas of the Christian life.

But when it comes to being a witness for Christ, you simply cannot fail! The only way you can fail to share Jesus effectively . . . is by not sharing him at all.

Yes, I Mean You!

Now, this is where people start to look at me funny. They get all jittery and jumpy. They see themselves floundering around, lost for answers, going blank on their Bible verses, and coming off looking like a big fool. They're scared to death that they'll try saying something and it'll come out all wrong.

Then they tell themselves they're going to change. (At least the ones who don't give up right away do.) They tell themselves they're going to get a better plan. They tell themselves they'll do better next time.

No, you won't do better next time. You won't change. You won't find a plan that finally fits every situation and works neatly around your schedule.

If you're going to do this, God's going to do it through you.

But guess what? That's where things get really encouraging, because God is simply too big, too great, and too in love with both you and the lost to mess this up. So everything good that's about to happen in your ministry as a Christian witness—and it *is* about to happen, I'm telling you—will come from God's Spirit working inside you.

It'll start when you sincerely pray, "Father, take away my fear, as well as anything else that's keeping me from sharing the gospel." For example:

• *Let him take away your excuses.* Never again fall for the line that you're not gifted enough to share your faith. Does God ever ask you to check and see if you're gifted in moral purity? Or in telling the truth? Or in reading his Word? Sharing Jesus is a clear command of Scripture, just like all these other things are. Don't you dare let the so-called qualified keep all the blessings to themselves!

• *Let him take away your pride.* It's our over-the-top concern for our own comfort, safety, and reputation that keeps us clammed up and uncaring. Let him take that self-centered side of you and smash it into a million pieces! When he picks you back up, you'll be just right for what he needs.

• *Let him take away your bad memories.* Don't let your seeming failures as a witness rob you of the joy that comes from fearlessly sharing Christ. Being turned down or turned away is not defeat. People are not rejecting you when they refuse to believe. They're rejecting Jesus!

You are not responsible for what people do with your love, care, and Christ-centered words. But you *are* responsible to share with them.

Get Fearless!

So, are you ready? Ready to start each day with no greater priority than being an ambassador for Christ? Ready to become more concerned about others' eternal destiny than you are about your own desire to read the newspaper, or run your errands, or keep to yourself? Ready to get involved with God, becoming part of his plan to forgive sins and to promise people forever?

Are you ready to see his grace pouring out on people right before your eyes?

Then let's get to praying.

That's what this journal is, really. *It's a prayer journal.* Even the parts of this book that are more informational in nature are meant to be received and read in prayer.

As you read, as you pray:

• God will help you discover a long, running list of people—people who are right within the flow of your average day—who are in need of Christ and might very well respond to a word from you.

• He'll help you start recognizing opportunities to share Jesus that you'd never even noticed before.

• He'll help you match biblical truths with observations from your own experience, giving your witness more than just chapters and verses but real-life conviction.

• He'll inspire you to take deliberate steps into people's lives, praying for them, pleading for their surrender to his will, and fearlessly sharing Jesus with them.

• He'll renew your heart, your mind, your will, your emotions—everything about you—transforming you into a bold, believable, responsive follower of Christ.

And I pray that this journal will be a big part of how he does it.

One More Thing

This is not necessarily the kind of book that you work through from start to finish. There are certain sections you'll want to jump ahead to or flip back for, and many more that you'll want to keep adding to as God takes the fear out of your faith.

I do encourage you to start, though, by looking at the worship and personal testimony sections that come next. They'll get you ready to go.

After that, the field is yours. I think you'll quickly find yourself at home in it.

The largest part of the book (by far) are the four big journaling sections that help you keep an ongoing log of answered prayers, God-opened opportunities, and lessons you're learning along the way. This is your place to pray out loud, make notes to yourself, and keep track of your journey. Don't let the blank pages intimidate you. Start filling them in with everything the Spirit is teaching you as you *share Jesus without fear!*

I, for one, am praying for you as you let God lead you into this exciting experience. You can be sure that he'll take you all the way!

OPEN UP IN WORSHIP

Take Time to Bow Down

One of the main reasons why we sometimes choke on our witnessing words is because we think sharing Jesus is all up to us. We tend to forget that when we're out there in the action, God is already actively involved, drawing people to himself . . . and steering us hard in each other's direction.

So use the next few journaling pages to reacquaint yourself with some things about God you may have forgotten or had let slip onto the back burner.

This is a big God we serve. And it's always a good time to remember that!

Lord, just stopping to think of you, so many words come to mind, so many reasons to praise and honor you . . . like your purity . . . your wisdom . . . your mercy . . . your unchangeableness . . .

_____

_____

_____

_____

_____

_____

_____

_____

_____

_____

_____

_____

_____

_____

_____

_____

_____

_____

_____

_____

_____

_____

_____

_____

_____

A few of the things you've written down probably strike you more strongly than others at the moment. For one reason or another, the Holy Spirit has made these pop out in your mind. So spend a few minutes praying through these choice characteristics of God, trying to sense from him why they may be of increased importance to you at this time in your life.

_____

_____

_____

_____

_____

_____

_____

_____

_____

_____

_____

_____

_____

_____

_____

_____

React now to these expressions of praise that flow so freely and confidently from those who already live in God's visible presence. Pray about anything that may be keeping you from letting things like these matter to you today:

Our Lord and God, You are worthy to receive glory and honor and power, because You have created all things, and because of Your will they exist and were created.

REVELATION 4:11

_____

_____

_____

_____

_____

_____

_____

The kingdom of the world has become the kingdom of our Lord and of His Messiah, and He will reign forever and ever! . . . We thank you, Lord God, the Almighty, who is and who was, because You have taken Your great power and have begun to reign.

REVELATION 11:15,17

The salvation and the power and the kingdom of our God and the authority of His Messiah have now come, because the accuser of our brothers has been thrown out: the one who accuses them before our God day and night. . . . Therefore rejoice, O heavens, and you who dwell in them!

REVELATION 12:10,12

Great and awe-inspiring are Your works, Lord God, the Almighty; righteous and true are Your ways, King of the Nations. Lord, who will not fear and glorify Your name? Because You alone are holy, because all the nations will come and worship before You, because Your righteous acts have been revealed.

REVELATION 15:3–4

Look! God's dwelling is with men, and He will live with them. They will be His people, and God Himself will be with them and be their God. He will wipe away every tear from their eyes. Death will exist no longer; grief, crying, and pain will exist no longer, because the previous things have passed away.

REVELATION 21:3–4

Before You Move On . . .

Let your worship and wonder explode onto these two pages (and into the margins and anywhere else you need to go to contain them). But make sure you don't leave this prayer until God has convinced you of his absolute splendor, his eternal power, and his ever-reaching love.

IT'S YOUR STORY

Live to Tell What God Has Done for You

Many of us simply assume that the story of our experience with God is far too boring, far too uneventful, far too little to convince anyone that he is all the things we've just been praying about.

The truth is, though, that nothing is quite as compelling as one life transformed by the power of Christ . . . not merely at the moment of conversion, but day by day, week after week, as God makes you into more than you ever were before.

So just to get the hang of this, what's one thing God has done to get your attention and to impact your life . . . in just the last week or so?

_____

_____

_____

_____

_____

_____

_____

_____

_____

_____

_____

_____

_____

_____

_____

_____

_____

_____

_____

Now . . . just to prove to you how easy it is to construct your own Christian testimony, I want you take *one minute* (that's probably all the time you'll need) to describe what your life was like before you met Christ . . .

_____

_____

_____

_____

_____

_____

_____

_____

_____

_____

_____

_____

_____

_____

_____

_____

_____

_____

_____

_____

_____

_____

_____

_____

_____

Okay. Now take *another* minute to describe how you became a Christian. How did it happen? What led up to it? Who was there? What did they say? How did you know this was real? How hard was it to respond? Who was the happiest when you told them? It's your story. You tell it.

_____

_____

_____

_____

_____

_____

_____

Finally, take one more minute to explain the difference Christ has made in your life since then. What do you do differently just because you're a Christian? Compare who you *could* be to the person you *are*—or at least the person you're praying God will keep changing you into.

_____

_____

_____

_____

_____

_____

_____

_____

_____

_____

_____

_____

_____

_____

_____

_____

_____

_____

_____

_____

_____

_____

_____

_____

_____

_____

See, wasn't that simple? There's your testimony! It's yours—nobody else's! And I'm telling you what—even if you're one of those who wasn't saved in bold, dramatic fashion, your story is perhaps even more so a testimony to the faithful goodness of God, who graciously kept you from ever experiencing the absolute worst that sin can do. Would you ask God to open a doorway for you to share this grand story of yours (and his) with someone soon?

_____

_____

_____

_____

_____

_____

_____

_____

_____

Before You Leave This Section . . .

Put your thanks into words of praise. Reconnect with the awesome grace that has given you your current standing with Christ. Tell him you're grateful for things like . . .

_____

_____

_____

_____

_____

_____

Pray also for your deepest desires, the places where you still have so much left to submit to Christ. He wants to have every bit of you under his control. Agree with him in prayer about this . . .

_____

_____

_____

_____

_____

_____

_____

_____

_____

_____

Pray about your many roles and relationships. How badly do you want God to use you through your family, through your work, through your church, and all the areas where you live—to be a light that points to Christ?

_____

_____

_____

_____

_____

_____

_____

Ask God to work through your own church—through all its members and ministries—to seek his will, know his heart, and share his love . . .

_____

_____

_____

_____

_____

_____

_____

_____

_____

_____

_____

YOU NEVER KNOW

A Real-Life Witnessing Story

I was flying back home one day in the fall of 2001. As soon as I had boarded the plane and found my seat, while everyone was starting to get settled in, I handed a gospel tract to one of the flight attendants as she happened by. "Why don't you read this while we're taking off?" I said.

Within a matter of minutes, she was back at my seat, obviously troubled and surprised. "Why did you give me this?" she asked, still holding the pamphlet in her hand. "You're the sixth person in two weeks who's handed me something like this!"

"Hmm," I said, waiting for more, wanting to see what the Spirit was doing.

Finally, she blurted out, "What does God want from me?" honestly wondering if I might know the answer.

"He wants your life," I calmly replied.

As tears began coming to her eyes, I asked if we could step into the galley to talk. I shared the Scriptures with her, told her about about the love of Christ, and she received him into her heart that very day.

Little did I know—little did she know—but thank God *he* knew—she would be serving passengers the next day, September 11, on a flight from Newark bound for San Francisco . . . that would crash in a field south of Pittsburgh.

You see, we never know who's crossing our path at any given time, on any given day. We may not know much if anything about them. We may not have the foggiest notion what has thrown us together at this particular moment.

But God knows. He knows where they've been, where they are, where they're going. And in his loving grace, he has brought them passing by our way today, where he knows that his Word is already housed in our hearts, tucked away and ready in our coat pockets, and within inches from this one he's been drawing to himself over time.

Seriously, you don't have to force yourself on them. That's neither your job nor your obligation. All you have to do is just be there. Just be you. Just be his. Don't be afraid.

PEOPLE I'M PRAYING FOR

Start Here, Go from There

When I ask most people to tell me who they're praying for to receive Christ, they usually give me a name or two. Maybe three.

Maybe none.

To be quite honest with you, the problem with most of us isn't that the people on our prayer list aren't coming to Christ. The problem is, *we don't even HAVE a prayer list!* We're not expending the simple energy even to consider the fact that people in our direct line of sight are lost and in need of a Savior.

Now, if hearing me say this feels like a step on the toes, then this is the place to start giving me a good reason to back off. I want you to start opening your heart up in prayer, and begin letting God fill—I mean, *fill*—the next few pages with a running list of people you can begin praying for today.

Sound impossible? Not really.

My good friend, Dave Bennett, has helped me more than anybody else in showing me that life puts us in touch—on a regular basis—with a lot more people than we realize. Even those of us who feel so insulated from non-Christians, who think we rarely come into contact with an unbeliever, would be amazed to discover how untrue that is.

Dave and a colleague of his, Richard Leach, have developed a grid of seven "neighborhoods," they call them—seven spheres of activity or relationship that your life naturally orbits around. Here they are.

So start your lists. Think them through. And stay tuned for further instructions.

1. Your relational neighborhood—people in your family, down to the ones you're related to through marriage or distant kin. This is usually our first place to recognize (and have access to) the names and faces of the unsaved.

	C	N	?
_____	C	N	?
_____	C	N	?
_____	C	N	?
_____	C	N	?
_____	C	N	?
_____	C	N	?
_____	C	N	?
_____	C	N	?
_____	C	N	?
_____	C	N	?
_____	C	N	?
_____	C	N	?
_____	C	N	?
_____	C	N	?
_____	C	N	?

2. Your geographical neighborhood—close friends, neighbors, roommates, landlords, renters, maybe the people who spray your house for bugs or cut your grass.

	C	N	?
_____	C	N	?
_____	C	N	?
_____	C	N	?

_____ C   N   ?

_____ C   N   ?

_____ C   N   ?

_____ C   N   ?

_____ C   N   ?

_____ C   N   ?

_____ C   N   ?

_____ C   N   ?

_____ C   N   ?

_____ C   N   ?

_____ C   N   ?

3. Your career neighborhood—coworkers, clients, the guy who delivers the mail to your office, people you drink coffee with, people affiliated with your industry, those you brush shoulders with from time to time.

_____ C   N   ?

_____ C   N   ?

_____ C   N   ?

_____ C   N   ?

_____ C   N   ?

_____ C   N   ?

_____ C   N   ?

_____ C   N   ?

_____ C   N   ?

_____ C   N   ?

_____ C N ?

_____ C N ?

_____ C N ?

_____ C N ?

_____ C N ?

_____ C N ?

4. *Your lifestyle neighborhood*—people you come across during your free time, like the sign-in clerk at the gym, acquaintances you know through clubs or organizations, folks you see at the laundromat or the recycling center, the guy who runs the pro shop at the golf course.

_____ C N ?

_____ C N ?

_____ C N ?

_____ C N ?

_____ C N ?

_____ C N ?

_____ C N ?

_____ C N ?

_____ C N ?

_____ C N ?

_____ C N ?

_____ C N ?

_____ C N ?

_____ C N ?

_____ C N ?

_____ C   N   ?

_____ C   N   ?

_____ C   N   ?

_____ C   N   ?

_____ C   N   ?

_____ C   N   ?

5. *Your retail neighborhood*—the Wal-Mart greeter, the people who scan your groceries and pack your bags, restaurant waiters, bank tellers, store associates, your doctors and nurses, your barber or hair stylist, your pharmacist, you get the picture. Even telemarketers!

_____ C   N   ?

_____ C   N   ?

_____ C   N   ?

_____ C   N   ?

_____ C   N   ?

_____ C   N   ?

_____ C   N   ?

_____ C   N   ?

_____ C   N   ?

_____ C   N   ?

_____ C   N   ?

_____ C   N   ?

_____ C   N   ?

_____ C   N   ?

_____ C   N   ?

_____ C N ?

_____ C N ?

_____ C N ?

_____ C N ?

6. Your highways-and-hedges neighborhood—people you'll probably only see once in a lifetime, but who you want to keep praying for: the man who was standing behind you in line at the polls, the couple you sat next to on an airplane. God knows them.

_____ C N ?

_____ C N ?

_____ C N ?

_____ C N ?

_____ C N ?

_____ C N ?

_____ C N ?

_____ C N ?

_____ C N ?

_____ C N ?

_____ C N ?

_____ C N ?

_____ C N ?

_____ C N ?

_____ C N ?

_____ C N ?

_____ C N ?

7. Your ministry neighborhood—these are the folks whose names come up during Sunday school class or on a Wednesday night prayer sheet. Keep adding their names here as a reminder to keep praying.

	C	N	?
_____	C	N	?
_____	C	N	?
_____	C	N	?
_____	C	N	?
_____	C	N	?
_____	C	N	?
_____	C	N	?
_____	C	N	?
_____	C	N	?
_____	C	N	?
_____	C	N	?
_____	C	N	?
_____	C	N	?
_____	C	N	?
_____	C	N	?
_____	C	N	?
_____	C	N	?
_____	C	N	?
_____	C	N	?
_____	C	N	?

Share Jesus Prayer Pointers

Now here's what I want you to do:

• *First, go back to each name you've written down*, and notice the C, N, and question mark beside each one. Next to each name, circle C if you know this person is a Christian; circle N if you know he or she is *not* a Christian; circle the question mark if you simply don't know. The idea here is to take as many people out of the "question mark" category as possible, which means you've actually shared enough with them to know the answer.

• *Second, begin praying regularly and specifically for the people on this list.* Nothing is more important than taking these precious names before the Father, asking him to work his will in their lives, and praying for the opportunity to be part of the way he does it.

• *Third, start being intentional about sharing Jesus with them.* We rarely get around to things we don't plan to do. So I encourage you—no, I absolutely *implore* you—to begin taking steps toward reaching them with the gospel. We'll talk later about some ways to do this, but make sure you're always fully available to the Holy Spirit, ready to invest yourself in these people's lives. Then keep track of what's happening, writing either in the margins around their names or in the many other journaling pages in this book.

• *Finally, keep adding to this list.* As the Lord leads you into contact with others—and he will, routinely—find a spot for each new name under one of these categories. Also, begin cultivating an attitude of watchfulness in every one of these "neighborhoods." The lost are out there. The harvest is plentiful. God just needs some good harvesters.

CONVERSATION STARTERS

How to Watch for an Open Door

I promise you, once you start looking for it to happen, God will come up in conversation without your even trying hard. It really doesn't take much for people to begin giving their opinion, exposing their need, and asking for help—not when the Spirit is working on them!

But the problem is, most of us have our heads down, content to shoot the breeze without letting the Lord lead our discussions. Remember, you can't fail when you're obeying God!

Try to think of a few openers of your own—some get-acquainted questions that can't easily be answered with a *yes* or *no*, but that express your genuine interest in someone . . . and open the floor for real dialogue.

-
-
-
-
-
-

Make a list of some of the subjects and interests you most like to talk about. How could you use them to open a door for witnessing?

- _____

- _____

- _____

- _____

- _____

What are some good ways to find out what makes *other* people tick, to find out in conversation what interests *them*?

- _____

- _____

- _____

- _____

- _____

Making the Switch

After the flow of conversation has started, you can use some specific questions to gauge another person's spiritual readiness, to see if they're close or far away. I call this "making the switch"—turning the conversation to spiritual matters.

Some people will be put off by this. That's fine. You've done your job, and I promise you—even though it may not seem like it now—your boldness to witness will continue having an impact in their lives.

But some of the people you ask will already be primed by the Spirit, and they'll want to keep going with you. These questions, then, are sort of like a meat thermometer, helping you determine whether or not God is at work here. Among the questions I like to use are:

1. *"Do you have any kind of spiritual beliefs?"*
   (Or "Do you go to church anywhere?")

2. *"Who is Jesus Christ to you?"*

3. *"Do you believe in heaven or hell?"*

4. *"If you died, where would you go?"*

5. *"If what you're believing isn't true, would you want to know?"*

Almost without fail, if you get to this point in talking with someone, you'll be able to start sharing Scriptures with them. *And that is the primary goal of a Jesus sharer!* Your main job as a witness is just to turn pages of the Bible. (We'll talk a little later in this book about a simple plan you can use for sharing Scripture very naturally with someone.)

But first, talk to the Lord about your desire to be made bold for Christ. Tell him what you mean when you say, "I'll do whatever you ask."

Lord, I ask for your own grace and courage to flow through me, caring enough to share Jesus with the people I meet, the people I know, and the people I'm around on an ongoing basis. Show me how to begin . . . and how to keep going . . .

SHARE JESUS
Journal

This is the first of three more sections just like this—wide-open spaces for you to make notes, write out prayers, jot reminders, scribble down verses, and basically get serious about sharing Jesus.

Over the next few weeks, I want to see these pages filling up with prayer requests, salvation celebrations, follow-up appointments, and whatever else God begins to do and teach as you let him break through your fears and into others' lives.

There are no rules here. No forms to fill out. No one way to do it. This is your response to what God is doing. This is your investment in people's hearts and minds. This is the true look of obedience.

You're going to be busy for a while, so I'll talk to you later.

We are ambassadors for Christ; certain that God is appealing through us, we plead on Christ's behalf, "Be reconciled to God."

2 CORINTHIANS 5:20

_____

_____

_____

_____

_____

_____

_____

_____

_____

_____

_____

"Many people came into my life over the years to share their faith, but I would not receive it. I sent them away discouraged, because I either insulted, antagonized, or persecuted them. I'm sure they felt like failures. But that's a lie. For I never forgot the name, the face, the person, or the words of anyone who ever told me about Jesus."

_____

_____

_____

_____

_____

_____

For by grace you are saved through faith, and this is not from yourselves; it is God's gift—not from works, so that no one can boast.

EPHESIANS 2:8–9

_____

_____

_____

_____

_____

_____

_____

_____

_____

_____

_____

_____

_____

"Consider ways you can serve the people on your prayer list. Help them with a needed task, like moving, or performing a difficult home project. Invite them over for a meal, or take them with you to a special event that you know they'd enjoy."

_____

_____

_____

"Nonbelievers must hear the gospel an average of 7.6 times before they receive it. So if anyone walks away from you when you share with them, remember: the Word of God never returns void. Be thankful you added your 1.0 to their lives. And pray for God to send others to take them the rest of the way."

Do nothing out of rivalry or conceit, but in humility consider others as more important than yourselves. Everyone should look out not only for his own interests, but also for the interests of others.

PHILIPPIANS 2:3–4

"A survey from the Institure of American Church Growth showed that 75 to 90 percent of new believers come to Christ through a friend or acquaintance who explains the good news on a one-to-one basis, as opposed to a church service or big event. Your personal witness is really huge."

Set your minds on what is above, not on what is on the earth. For you have died, and your life is hidden with the Messiah in God.

COLOSSIANS 3:2–3

"How in the world can you reach someone who can't understand God's love? Guess what: you can't. That's the job of the Holy Spirit. But the Holy Spirit moves through God's Word, and you can make sure they get to hear that."

BY A NOSE

A Real-Life Prayer Story

I was in the Denver airport (seems like I'm always in the airport), only this time it was 5:00 A.M. and my flight had been delayed.

Oh, great.

So I headed for the frequent flyer room, wondering what God had in store. I knew he might have his own good reason for stranding me there for the next few hours. But as I went in and found a seat, I didn't see anyone around. It looked like it was just me and Jesus, all by ourselves.

Within a few seconds, though, I realized I was wrong. There *was* somebody else in there. One guy . . . with a whiskey bottle. A coffee cup. A guitar leaning against the chair next to him. If you'd have been there, you'd have seen him too. *And you'd have known exactly who he was.*

Still, I waited. I prayed. But the Spirit wasn't letting up. In fact, somewhere deep in my heart, I decided this encounter called for a drive-by, a shocker, a tactic I only use when I'm very sure the Lord is directing me to do it.

I got up from my chair, walked over to where this man was sitting, and asked, "Are you Mr. (blank)?" He hopped straight up and looked me square in the eye. "Hey!" he said, "I haven't seen you in a couple of days." (He'd never seen me in his life.)

"No," I answered, "but I am a man who's prayed for you for five years. And I have a message from your dead father: 'Why aren't you flying in your private jet? Isn't Craig still your pilot? And how are your three children?" (I mentioned them by name.)

How, you're wondering, (he too was wondering) did I have all that information?

In the height of my pagan lifestyle, this man's father had been my copilot on the Lear jet that flew me all over the country, doing business for the Mafia. We had talked many times about his famous son. I knew their family situation well. Yes, even while I was involved in the most ungodly activities you can imagine, God was already at work in my life, preparing me for just such a moment as this one.

A Real-Life Prayer Story (continued)

Nine years after my own conversion, I held the hand of this gentleman—the father of the man in the airport—as he confessed Christ. He asked me at the time if I'd ever be willing to share Jesus with his boy. I told him that if God provided the opportunity, it would be my privilege. But I didn't know how he would ever bring it about. It wasn't like I had access into the man's life.

Until right this minute.

— — —

The first person I called after this airport encounter was my friend Kathie Grant, who is without a doubt the most dedicated prayer warrior I know. "Kathie," I said, "I just met (this person) at the airport. Have you been praying for him?"

She answered, "Not only have I been praying for him—for sixteen years—but four days ago the Spirit led me to pray that you'd meet him at the airport!"

I knew it. God was at work.

Soon after I returned home, I also made mention of this to one of my neighbors, Cheryl, who I must say is one of the shyest Christians I have ever been around. The first time I met her, I was out cutting the grass when I spotted her walking by, wheeling her newborn son, David, in a stroller. I stopped the mower, started to get acquainted, and asked her if she was a Christian. "Yes," she answered, not looking me in the eye, but sort of gazing off at about the level of my gutters.

So I said, "Great, wait here just a second," while I hollered up to John, a repairman who was right at that moment up on my roof. John came down the ladder, walked over to where Cheryl and I were standing, and I said to him, "John, this is Cheryl. She's new to the neighborhood, and she's a Christian. She's going to tell you how to receive Jesus."

I walked off. Cheryl could have killed me.

But before their conversation was over, John had given his life to Christ.

So I told Cheryl about what had happened to me in the airport, and who I had shared Jesus with. She said, "You don't know this, but God has been leading me to pray for him for some time, and I've been weeping over his name every time I do. What's going on here?"

The next day, I was in Salina, Kansas, leading a conference. One of the men there was Dr. Roy Moody, state director of evangelism. I told him we needed to get some people together to pray for this individual I had spoken to.

"Just a minute," Roy said, heading over to the telephone. He rang up a friend, Abe, an Oklahoma state legislator and born-again Christian. I didn't know it, but these two had been praying together for a long time that the Lord would bring someone into the life of Abe's well-known nephew, someone who would share Jesus with him. Now God was beginning to connect the dots.

"It's on!" Roy announced excitedly into the receiver.

— — —

Yes, it was. For two solid hours in the Denver airport, this man read every verse I showed him. There wasn't one Scripture he didn't understand . . . and not one he would accept. Finally, I asked, "When did you make up your mind that you wouldn't be a Christian?"

"I was twelve years old," he answered. "A Sunday school teacher told me that Jesus was the way, the truth, and the life. And I said to myself at that moment that he would never be for me."

This guy just wouldn't believe. He would not accept Christ as Savior. And within a matter of weeks, he was dead, tragically killed.

— — —

Wasn't what you expected, was it? Not every story has a happy ending.

But I really struggled to understand this one. I remember asking God, "Why all this trouble? Why take up Kathie's and Cheryl's and Roy's and Abe's and all of our praying time on him? Why put me into this guy's life one-on-one where he could hear all these Scriptures? Why didn't this end in a celebration?"

A verse came to me soon thereafter that has had a great impact on my life. I hope it will for you. "For we are to God the aroma of Christ among those who are being saved *and* those who are perishing [dying]. To the one we are the smell of death; to the other, the fragrance of life" (2 Cor. 2:15–16, NIV).

We are ambassadors of Christ to all men, even those who are dying. Because let me remind you that "death," when used in Scripture, often means eternal separation from God. It's not up to us to know what *kind* of "aroma" we're giving off at a particular moment. It's just up to us to *be* the "aroma of Christ." And to God be all the glory!

PRAYING THE WORD

Two Powers, Put Together

I am totally convinced that our main reason for fear—our main reason for *ever* getting spiritually confused and off-course—is because we neglect to spend time reading and heeding the Word of God. He has given us this treasure to communicate his will to us, to define for us what's true and what's not, and to express his heart's desire for the people of the world.

And whenever we add prayer into the mix, combining our pleas to God with the assurances of Scripture, we are on the trail of something truly powerful!

Kathie Grant, whose intense passion for Christ was so pivotal in my own conversion, is a living testimony to this. Throughout the course of any given day, she will pray for literally thousands of people—deliberately, individually—always anchoring her requests to clear passages from the Bible that relate to their situations.

In her book, *Praying in the Word of God*, Kathie shares how she prays for the lost in this way. I invite you to begin doing this yourself in the pages that follow. Read the verse, begin with the prayer starter, then fashion your own prayers for the hearts of the unsaved.

He saved us—not by works of righteousness that we had done, but according to His mercy.

TITUS 3:5

Dear heavenly Father, just as you saved us because of your mercy, save our loved ones. Forgive us, those who already believe, of our self-righteousness. For we were once just like the lost, and it was your mercy, not our righteousness, that saved us . . .

_____

_____

_____

_____

_____

_____

_____

_____

For Your faithful love is higher than the heavens; Your faithfulness reaches the clouds.

PSALM 108:4

Dear heavenly Father, we believe and trust in your character—your love that is higher than the heavens and your faithfulness that reaches the skies—to save those who do not believe. Only because of your faithful love can anyone find salvation . . .

_____

_____

_____

_____

_____

_____

_____

_____

He Himself is the propitiation for our sins, and not only for ours, but also for those of the whole world.

1 JOHN 2:2

Dear heavenly Father, since you have given Christ as an atoning sacrifice for the sins of the whole world, we apply his sacrifice to every nation on earth, and we pray that many within each nation will come to believe in him, just as we do . . .

_____

_____

_____

_____

_____

_____

_____

Whoever calls on the name of the Lord will be saved.

ACTS 2:21

Dear merciful Father, how gracious you are that all sinners have to do is call on the name of your Son! That is because he has paid the price for everyone. Enable sinners to call, and send out believers to tell of his name . . .

_____

_____

_____

_____

_____

_____

_____

_____

_____

_____

_____

*I am the good shepherd. I know my own sheep, and they know Me. . . .
But I have other sheep that are not of this fold; I must bring them also.*

JOHN 10:14,16

*Dear Great Shepherd, call your other sheep, those who have not
yet received you, for you have promised that they will hear you.
Bring them into the flock, and make us one with you . . .*

The god of this age has blinded the minds of the unbelievers
so they cannot see the light of the gospel of the glory of Christ.

2 Corinthians 4:4

Dear Father, please have mercy on unbelievers, just as you did on us before we believed. We too were at one time blinded by the devil. But in your mercy, you took the blindness from our minds so that we could believe in Christ and be saved. Do the same for unbelievers everywhere . . .

*No one can come to Me unless the Father who sent Me draws him,
and I will raise him up on the last day.*

JOHN 6:44

*Dear heavenly Father, according to this verse, no one can come
to Christ unless you enable him. Therefore, we pray that you will
draw unbelievers to Christ, enabling them to believe in him, your
precious Son, and raising them up on the last day . . .*

_____

_____

_____

_____

_____

_____

_____

The Son is not able to do anything on His own, but only what He sees the Father doing.

JOHN 5:19

Dear heavenly Father, if the Son of God could do nothing by himself but only what he saw you doing, then how much more must we look to see what you are doing! And because you love us as you love the Son, you will show us all you are doing . . .

_____

_____

_____

_____

_____

_____

_____

_____

_____

_____

_____

WHY SO AFRAID?

Where Fears Go to Die

After many years of equipping Christians to share their faith, I've narrowed down the most common witnessing fears to six. Let's look at them for a second. Let's talk to God about them in prayer. Then let's watch him blow them away!

1. "I'm afraid of being rejected."

Lord, the apostle Paul said in 1 Thessalonians 4:8 that those who reject your truth do "not reject man, but God." So I ask you to help me look at my fear from this perspective . . .

_____

_____

_____

_____

_____

_____

_____

_____

_____

_____

_____

_____

_____

_____

_____

_____

2. "I'm afraid of what my friends will think."

Lord God, I know from John 15:20 that "a slave is not greater than his master. If they persecuted [Jesus], they will also persecute [me]." Teach me how to walk boldly and unashamedly in this truth . . .

_____

_____

_____

_____

_____

_____

_____

_____

_____

_____

_____

_____

_____

_____

_____

_____

_____

_____

_____

_____

3. "I don't think I can share with my coworkers."

Father, when you tell us to "always be ready to give a defense to anyone who asks you for a reason for the hope that is in you" (1 Pet. 3:15), I'm assuming you didn't say "always" by accident . . .

_____

_____

_____

_____

_____

_____

_____

_____

_____

_____

_____

_____

_____

_____

_____

_____

_____

_____

_____

_____

_____

_____

_____

4. "I don't know enough."

Lord, you must have instructed Paul, who admitted to being "in much trembling," not to worry about using "persuasive words of wisdom," but simply to demonstrate the Spirit's power (1 Cor. 2:3–4). That's what I want to do, God . . .

_____

_____

_____

_____

_____

_____

_____

_____

_____

_____

_____

_____

_____

5. "I'm afraid of losing my friends and relatives."

As hard as this is to swallow, Lord, I know you said in Matthew 10:37, "The person who loves father or mother . . . son or daughter more than Me is not worthy of Me." Help me, Lord, to love both them and you enough to share Jesus with them . . .

6. "I don't know how."

When Moses blubbered about being inadequate, Lord, you told him, "I will certainly be with you" (Exod. 3:12). Be with me, Father, and teach me how to use your Word to share your love . . .

_____

_____

_____

_____

_____

_____

_____

_____

_____

_____

_____

_____

_____

_____

_____

_____

_____

_____

_____

_____

_____

_____

SHARE JESUS
Journal

This space is here—again—whenever you need it, to keep a running record of God's activity in your life. Use it well. And use it up.

_____

_____

_____

_____

_____

_____

_____

_____

_____

_____

_____

_____

_____

_____

_____

_____

_____

_____

_____

_____

_____

_____

_____

A word spoken at the right time is like golden apples on a silver tray.

PROVERBS 25:11

"Your motivation for evangelism must be your love for God and love for people. This is not a thing you are doing. This is not something that makes you superior to others. It is an act of consecration and belief in Jesus Christ."

Through Him, we have obtained access by faith into this grace in which we stand, and we rejoice in the hope of the glory of God.

ROMANS 5:2

_____

_____

_____

"Introduce your pre-Christian friends to your Christian friends in a non-threatening situation. In meeting believers, help them see for themselves that Christianity is embraced by all kinds of interesting people."

_____

_____

_____

_____

_____

_____

_____

_____

_____

_____

_____

_____

_____

_____

We cared so much for you that we were pleased to share with you not only the gospel of God but also our own lives, because you had become dear to us.

1 THESSALONIANS 2:8

"We need to be ready to offer more than just tidbits of truth to people. We can't be satisfied by saying to someone, 'God bless you,' or 'I'll be praying for you.' We must be prepared to share the whole gospel with them."

Even when I am old and gray, God, do not abandon me. Then I will proclaim Your power to another generation, Your strength to all who are to come.

PSALM 71:18

_____

_____

_____

_____

_____

_____

_____

_____

_____

_____

_____

_____

_____

_____

_____

_____

_____

_____

_____

_____

_____

_____

_____

_____

_____

_____

_____

_____

_____

_____

_____

_____

_____

_____

_____

_____

_____

_____

_____

"I can't make you a promise your fear will completely go away, but I can assure you that it will get easier. I promise you that your faith in God will go to an entirely new level as you share your faith."

Restore the joy of Your salvation to me, and give me a willing spirit. Then I will teach the rebellious Your ways, and sinners will return to You.

PSALM 51:12–13

COME AGAIN?

A Real-Life Witnessing Story

I lead *Share Jesus Without Fear* seminars all over the world. They're all such a treat to me. But I keep thinking I'll eventually get to the point where I've seen everything happen in one of my conferences that possibly could.

This, however, was a new one.

On this particular day, there were somewhere between 600 and 800 people in the audience. And when I gave the participants their assignment—to commit to using the five "Share Jesus" questions with someone that week—one man raised his hand.

"If I haven't come to Christ yet, can I still do the assignment?"

All the noise rushed out of the room. How was I going to answer this one?

"Where are you stuck, sir?" I asked him.

"I don't know," he said.

I stood there for about thirty seconds. I prayed for wisdom. I asked the Holy Spirit for direction. Then I stepped down from the podium, walked over to where the man was sitting, and began asking *him* the final five "Share Jesus" questions, one after the other.

"Are you a sinner?" Yes.

"Do you want forgiveness of sins?" Yes.

"Do you believe Jesus died on the cross for you and rose again?" Yes.

"Are you willing to surrender your life to Jesus Christ?" Yes.

"Are you ready to invite Jesus into your life and into your heart?" Yes.

"I've got news for you, friend. You're not stuck." He received Christ right there, in front of hundreds of cheering brothers and sisters. And the next Sunday, he and his (formerly) Buddhist wife were baptized together and received into the church.

Anything can happen. And we've got to be ready to capture the moment God creates . . . even if it's the last thing we'd expect.

PRAYING THE WILL OF GOD

Assure Yourself a Life Full of "Yes's"

God has revealed his will to us through his Word. Yes, as the apostle Peter came right out and admitted, "There are some matters that are hard to understand" (2 Pet. 3:16). Yet everything God needs us to know is clearly spelled out in the Bible, so that anyone can get it.

Don't be troubled, however, when your mind can't totally grasp God's will and his plan. If you could, what kind of God would that be! Still, we can ask him to teach us by his Holy Spirit, equipping us with all the understanding necessary for today.

So I invite you to continue praying through the Scriptures, seeking Christ's mercy for the lost, asking him to open their eyes to see his love, grace, and forgiveness poured out on them. This, we know, is his will. And this is our prayer.

For God loved the world in this way: He gave His One and Only Son, so that everyone who believes in Him will not perish but have eternal life.

JOHN 3:16

Dear loving Father, we pray that you will enable those who do not yet believe in Christ to have faith in him. May your love in sending Jesus be received by many people . . .

_____

_____

_____

_____

_____

_____

_____

_____

_____

_____

_____

_____

_____

The Spirit of the Lord is on Me, because He has anointed Me to preach good news to the poor. He has sent Me to proclaim freedom to the captives and recovery of sight to the blind, to set free the oppressed, to proclaim the year of the Lord's favor.

LUKE 4:18–19

Lord Jesus, just as you spoke these words from Isaiah 61 at the beginning of your personal ministry, we know this continues to be your will and desire. We pray that we who are your body will also proclaim the good news of the Lord's favor . . .

_____

_____

_____

It is I who sweep away your transgressions for My own sake and remember your sins no more.

Isaiah 43:25

Dear heavenly Father, it is for your own sake that you blot out the transgressions of family members, friends, and neighbors who come to believe in you. Though many of them do not yet believe, I pray for the day when through faith they can say of you that you remember their sins no more, for the sake of Christ Jesus . . .

Yahweh is a compassionate and gracious God, slow to anger and rich in faithful love and truth, maintaining faithful love to a thousand generations, forgiving wrongdoing, rebellion, and sin.

EXODUS 34:6–7

Heavenly Father, forgive thousands today because you are gracious, abounding in love and faithfulness. Take the lost as your inheritance, because of your worthiness . . .

But how can they call on Him in whom they have not believed? And how can they believe without hearing about Him? And how can they hear without a preacher?

ROMANS 10:14

Dear heavenly Father, send born-again Christians out to tell the gospel today, because sinners will not believe in Christ if they haven't heard of him and what he has done. May our faith in you compel us to make known the truth . . .

_____

_____

_____

_____

_____

_____

_____

_____

_____

_____

_____

This is good, and it pleases God our Savior, who wants everyone to be saved and to come to the knowledge of the truth.

1 TIMOTHY 2:3–4

Dear heavenly Father, You want all men to know this truth: that Christ gave himself as a ransom for us. Therefore, we apply your will and Christ's work to all the people on our prayer lists, asking you to give them the gift of faith . . .

_____

_____

_____

_____

_____

_____

_____

_____

_____

_____

Whenever we ask anything according to His will, He hears us. And if we know that He hears whatever we ask, we know that we have what we have asked Him for.

1 JOHN 5:14–15

Dear heavenly Father, we know you will answer our prayers for the lost, for we know that it is your will that none should perish. So we lift up the names of the people we love, believing that you hear us, believing that you will save them . . .

_____

_____

_____

_____

_____

_____

_____

_____

_____

_____

_____

_____

_____

_____

_____

_____

Whatever You ask in My name, I will do it so that the Father may be glorified in the Son.

JOHN 14:13

Lord Jesus, bring glory to the Father by doing what we ask of you, by saving our loved ones as well as others from every nation of the world. We feel perfect freedom in praying this because . . .

_____

_____

_____

_____

_____

_____

_____

_____

_____

_____

_____

_____

_____

Go, therefore, and make disciples of all nations, baptizing them in the name of the Father and of the Son and of the Holy Spirit.

MATTHEW 28:19

Dear Lord, we know that this command you gave to your first followers remains in force for us today. Fill your disciples with a passion to obey, and also with the Holy Spirit—that we may experience your presence and go in your authority . . .

SHARING THE SCRIPTURE

Getting Yourself out of the Way

People are rarely if ever brought to Christ by our convincing arguments and heady logic. The whole thing is in the hands of the Holy Spirit. If you lay the Scriptures out there where people can read them, God will do the rest.

Here's the basic model I use. You can certainly modify and personalize your own presentation, choosing different verses than these if you like. I'm not here to regulate the way you witness or insist that you do it a certain way. We're not taking medicine here. *We're sharing Christ!* But I would ask you to consider two very important things. Both of these principles are grounded in Scripture and are therefore biblically ordained to be highly effective:

1. When you share Scripture with someone, have him or her read the verse out loud. "Faith comes from hearing" (Rom. 10:17, NIV). More than anything, our job as sharers is to let the Scripture do the talking.

2. Ask this question after the person has read the Scripture verse: "What does it say to you?" Witnessing is not about telling people what you believe. It's about the Holy Spirit revealing truth through his Word. One time when an expert in the law came to Jesus, asking him for his opinion, Jesus replied, *"What is written in the law? How do you read it?"* (Luke 10:36). If this approach worked for Jesus, it should work for us.

So here are the seven verses I most often turn to when sharing Christ. I mark each one in a yellow highlighter so the other person can easily spot them. Then at the top of the page—written upside down, so that it reads correctly to me when my Bible is turned away from me—I write the reference of the next verse I'm going to turn to. This way, I don't even have to remember it!

And one more thing: I use a small sharing Bible when I'm witnessing, like the *Share Jesus Without Fear New Testament.* A big Bible is very intimidating. If I was an unbeliever and you took me to lunch, I'd have a hard enough time just being there with *you,* much less with you and *it*—your big, heavy study Bible. Just be considerate of others. Then here we go . . .

1. *"For all have sinned and fall short of the glory of God" (Rom. 3:23).*

Again, you're going to want to ask the people you're sharing with, "What do you think this means?" So put yourself in their shoes for a minute. What does this verse say to you?

_____

_____

_____

_____

_____

_____

_____

2. *"For the wages of sin is death, but the gift of God is eternal life in Christ Jesus our Lord" (Rom. 6:23).*

Same question. What are the "wages of sin"? What is the "gift of God"? Write it out. Talk in terms of your own sin—the sin which would have guaranteed you an eternity in hell if not for this "gift of God."

_____

_____

_____

_____

_____

_____

_____

_____

3. "I assure you: Unless someone is born again, he cannot see the kingdom of God" (John 3:3).

After reading Romans 6:23, I ask them, "Would you like to know how you can receive this gift of God?" That's when I turn to John 3:3. But then I do something a little different. I don't follow up with the "What does this say to you?" question. Instead I ask, "What did Jesus come to die for?" So I ask you: what does being "born again" do to our sin problem?

_____

_____

_____

_____

_____

_____

4. "I am the way, the truth, and the life. No one comes to the Father except through Me" (John 14:6).

This "one way" seems unfair to some. But how else can you read this verse? What else can it possibly mean? Yet those who reject Christ are hoping for some other way to get into heaven. You'll hear these ideas sometimes when people read this verse. So this is a good time to say to them, "Read it again." If they don't give you the obvious answer, keep telling them, "Read it again."

_____

_____

_____

_____

_____

5. *"If you confess with your mouth, 'Jesus is Lord,' and believe in your heart that God raised him from the dead, you will be saved" (Rom. 10:9).*

Can it really be this easy? Would you expect someone to be surprised how open the door really is? Yet people have a hard time believing they can be forgiven. "Read it again. What does it say to you?"

_____

_____

_____

_____

_____

6. *"He died for all so that those who live should no longer live for themselves, but for the One who died for them and was raised" (2 Cor. 5:15).*

What makes this prospect so freeing? What problems does this deal with?

_____

_____

_____

_____

7. *"Listen! I stand at the door and knock. If anyone hears My voice and opens the door, I will come in to him and have dinner with him, and he with Me" (Rev. 3:20).*

What is Jesus asking us to do? What happens to us when Jesus comes in?

_____

_____

_____

DECISION TIME

Let God Take It Home

Surprisingly enough, many of the people who might say "yes" to Jesus in the midst of a witnessing encounter will never do anything else with it. Unless they're encouraged to seek out the people who have been praying for them, to get connnected with a church, or to start reading God's Word, they may simply become more hardened or confused than ever.

After sharing the Scriptures with someone, after sensing the Spirit working in their hearts, ask the following five questions:

1. "Are you a sinner?"

This is based, of course, on the Romans 3:23 passage.

2. "Do you want forgiveness for your sins?"

Remember what Romans 6:23 said about the "wages" of sin.

3. "Do you believe Jesus died on the cross for you and rose again?"

This reaffirmation of Romans 10:9–11 helps them see why belief is necessary.

4. "Are you willing to surrender your heart to Jesus Christ?"

Jesus told people to count the cost. That makes this an important question.

5. "Are you ready to invite Jesus into your life and into your heart?"

When you get to this question, it's a good time to just stay quiet. In fact, if it didn't sound so ugly, I'd tell you to *shut up*—simply because that language carries the intensity I'm trying to get across. This is serious. God is working. Don't get in the way.

If a person answers "no," however, I have a special one-word answer that often makes a huge difference. My one word is: "Why?"

I remember a time when a certain businessman told me he just wasn't ready to receive Christ yet. So I asked him, "Why?" He continued to come up with answers and excuses, to which I continued to respond, "Okay, but why?" Pretty soon it was even becoming obvious to *him* that his logic was spiraling down into silliness. After falling silent for a moment, he finally looked me dejectedly in the eye and said, "I'm not making any sense at all, am I?"

"Nope," I answered. "So are you ready to give your life to Christ now?"

He was. And he did.

Why is "Why?" such a great witnessing tool?

_____

_____

_____

_____

_____

_____

_____

_____

_____

_____

_____

_____

SHARE JESUS
Journal

Just think—it won't be long (if it isn't happening already) before you're praising God on these pages for how he's beautifully brought people to Christ through your faithful sharing of the gospel. What started out as a fearsome, impossible task is being transformed by the Holy Spirit into a big, heaven-bound celebration! You just watch!

_____

_____

_____

_____

_____

_____

_____

_____

_____

_____

_____

_____

_____

_____

_____

_____

_____

_____

_____

_____

Don't worry about anything, but in everything, through prayer and petition with thanksgiving, let your requests be made known to God. And the peace of God, which surpasses every thought, will guard your hearts and your minds in Christ Jesus.

PHILIPPIANS 4:6–7

"Wait until you see what God will do with an ordinary person—like you, like me—when we are obedient in sharing our faith."

. . . *keeping our eyes on Jesus, the source and perfecter of our faith, who for the joy that lay before Him endured a cross and despised the shame, and has sat down at the right hand of God's throne.*

HEBREWS 12:2

"You may be afraid to witness for fear that people will ask questions you can't answer. But what would be wrong with responding, 'I don't know the answer to your question, but I'll try to find out'? If they really want to know and aren't just being difficult, they'll wait. Never let that throw you."

Dear friends, let us love one another, because love is from God, and everyone who loves has been born of God and knows God.

1 John 4:7

_____

_____

_____

_____

_____

_____

_____

_____

_____

_____

_____

_____

_____

_____

_____

_____

_____

_____

_____

_____

_____

"Often people are very willing to talk openly about their troubles. When this happens, the first thing we must do is listen, because the principle behind listening is love. We are not only listening to what someone is saying; we are listening to what God is saying. We are listening to find the best way to love this person."

You are called to freedom, brothers; only don't use this freedom as an opportunity for the flesh, but serve one another through love. For the entire law is fulfilled in one statement: "Love your neighbor as yourself."

GALATIANS 5:13–14

"I have learned a very simple way to recognize when God has decided it's time for me to write or call or to make a personal contact with someone from my past. I do this whenever that person's name comes to my mind. God's timing is always better than mine."

When the Spirit of truth comes, He will guide you into all the truth....
He will glorify Me, because He will take from what is Mine and declare
it to you.

JOHN 16:13–14

PRAYING THE PROMISES

Look Who's Got You Covered

By now you know that I put great stock in the Bible. Like you, I've seen for myself that the teachings of Scripture never grow old, never fail, and never come up needing a tweak or retraction to make them more accurate.

These promises are in the book, and they're here to stay.

So don't feel the need to rush through these. Instead, stop and savor every one. As you pray each promise back to God, let the Spirit take as long as he wants to draw out each word and nuance, each insight and outcome.

Put these promises in your heart, then walk them out in your life . . . and share them as you go.

Who will harm you if you are passionate for what is good? But even if you should suffer for righteousness, you are blessed.

1 PETER 3:13–14

Dear Lord, I know that as I go out to share your Word, I will be tempted to fear. But who can harm me? And even if they do, I am just as sure that you will transform their rejection into blessing, even their cursings into shouts of joy . . .

_____

_____

_____

_____

_____

_____

_____

_____

_____

_____

_____

_____

_____

_____

*The LORD said to him, "Who made the human mouth? Who makes him
mute or deaf, seeing or blind? Is it not I, the LORD? Now go! I will help
you speak and I will teach you what to say."*

EXODUS 4:11–12

*Dear heavenly Father, I give you my mouth, my steps, all my
activities of the day, and I ask you to be true to your Word—
to teach me what to say and help me to speak . . .*

_____

_____

_____

_____

_____

_____

_____

_____

_____

_____

Make up your mind not to prepare your defense ahead of time, for I will give you such words and a wisdom that none of your adversaries will be able to resist or contradict.

Luke 21:14–15

Lord Jesus, my mind is fixed on you, not on my fears. My heart is trusting in your ability to give me not only your words but also your wisdom, to speak your love and power through me . . .

You will receive power when the Holy Spirit has come upon you, and you will be My witnesses in Jerusalem, in all Judea and Samaria, and to the ends of the earth.

ACTS 1:8

Holy Spirit of God, I pray that you will come upon me in such power and purpose, in such strength and holy conviction, that your word in me will translate to meet the need of every person I talk to—wherever they come from, wherever they are . . .

_____

_____

_____

_____

_____

I am not ashamed of the gospel, because it is God's power for salvation to everyone who believes.

ROMANS 1:16

Dear Father, may I never fail to be grateful for the salvation you have given me, may I always be honored to bear your name, and may the promise of your salvation become love in my heart for all people everywhere . . .

_____

_____

_____

_____

_____

_____

_____

_____

_____

_____

_____

_____

If anyone is in Christ, there is a new creation; old things have passed away, and look, new things have come.

2 CORINTHIANS 5:17

Dear heavenly Father, help me never forget what I was like in my old ways. And when I see others acting from the nature of their old man, may I not judge. May I see instead the possibility of something new . . .

To those who are perishing, the message of the cross is foolishness, but to us who are being saved, it is God's power.

1 CORINTHIANS 1:18

Dear Lord, I know that there is much in the gospel that makes no sense to a human way of thinking. Yet I know it is true, and I believe in its power, and I ask for your favor in sharing this life-giving message every day . . .

I am not ashamed, because I know whom I have believed and am persuaded that He is able to guard what has been entrusted to me until that day.

2 TIMOTHY 1:12

Lord God, I pray that my confidence may always rest in you. I thank you for assuring us in your Word that nothing can stop the steady march of your kingdom, and that everyone you draw to yourself is safe for eternity . . .

COMMON OBJECTIONS

Let Me Explain

People will raise questions when you're sharing Jesus with them, sometimes out of a habit for being difficult and irritating, but often out of a genuine desire to understand. Still, you never want to get into an argument with someone. And you never want to sink to the level of just trying to win your point. The goal of all this is to share Jesus. In love. Right?

But that doesn't mean others won't have a difference of opinion about certain matters during a spiritual conversation. Here, in fact, are the ten objections I've most commonly come up against. Write out your own responses to these objections—not whole treatises or anything, just a few notes and comments— or better yet, Bible verses. Later on, when you think of something else, come back and add that, too.

1. "I'm not ready."

_____

_____

_____

_____

_____

_____

_____

_____

_____

2. *"My friends will think I'm crazy if I accept Jesus."*

_____

_____

_____

_____

_____

_____

_____

_____

_____

_____

3. *"What about my family? What will they think?"*

_____

_____

_____

_____

_____

_____

_____

_____

_____

_____

4. *"I've done too many bad things."*

_____

_____

_____

_____

_____

_____

_____

_____

_____

5. *"I'm having too much fun."*

_____

_____

_____

_____

_____

_____

_____

_____

_____

6. *"Why does God let bad things happen?"*

_____

_____

_____

_____

_____

_____

_____

_____

_____

_____

7. *"There are many paths to God."*

_____

_____

_____

_____

_____

_____

_____

_____

_____

_____

8. *"There are many religions in the world."*

_____

_____

_____

_____

_____

_____

_____

_____

_____

9. *"I've always believed in God."*

_____

_____

_____

_____

_____

_____

_____

_____

_____

10. "There are too many hypocrites in the church."

_____

_____

_____

_____

_____

_____

_____

_____

_____

_____

_____

_____

Actually, I list not only these ten but a total of thirty-six common objections to the gospel as an appendix in my book, *Share Jesus Without Fear.* For each one, I give you a script to use—a simple, suggested response—to help you avoid the distractions that detours and rabbit trails can cause. I hope you'll check it out.

SHARE JESUS
Journal

This is the last section of this book, this prayer journal. But it's just the beginning of what God is going to continue doing through you as you share Jesus without fear! I know you will not want to stop here, so I pray that this discipline—keeping track of your witnessing experiences—will become a lifelong pursuit and passion of yours.

You will be in my prayers as you live out this command and privilege, as you take eternal life with you every day into your world. *"I pray that you may be active in sharing your faith, so that you will have a full understanding of every good thing we have in Christ" (Philem. 6, NIV).*

And be sure to spread the message around, bringing other believers on board, encouraging them in sharing their faith, letting God use you to make a real difference. So get ready! Your sharing experiences are sure to come, because God always answers obedience. Remember: *you cannot fail!*

_____

_____

_____

_____

_____

_____

_____

_____

_____

_____

_____

_____

_____

From Him you are in Christ Jesus, who for us became wisdom from God, as well as righteousness, sanctification, and redemption, in order that, as it is written: "The one who boasts must boast in the Lord."

1 CORINTHIANS 1:30–31

"I can't think of a single time, out of the thousands of times I have shared my faith, that I haven't prayed for the person beforehand. Even if it is a chance meeting, I silently pray for God's help."

This Spirit He poured out on us abundantly through Jesus Christ our Savior, so that having been justified by His grace, we may become heirs with the hope of eternal life.

TITUS 3:6–7

"We want God to use us as spiritual magnets to attract others to himself. And this will happen only when we are living in a prayer relationship with him. We will have that sparkle in our eyes that reveals the joy of our hearts, that will make others jealous to want it for themselves."

Let the message about the Messiah dwell richly among you . . .
And whatever you do, in word or in deed, do everything in the name
of the Lord Jesus, giving thanks to God the Father through Him.

COLOSSIANS 3:16–17

_____

_____

_____

_____

_____

_____

_____

_____

_____

_____

_____

_____

_____

_____

_____

_____

_____

_____

_____

"Every morning during my quiet time, I ask God to give me the privilege of sharing Jesus with somebody whose heart is ready to hear the good news. That way, I spend my day on alert, constantly asking, 'Lord, is this the one you have sent me to today?' Always be looking for where he wants you to be."

He said to me, "My grace is sufficient for you, for power is perfected in weakness." Therefore, I will most gladly boast all the more about my weaknesses, so that Christ's power may reside in me.

2 CORINTHIANS 12:9

"Evangelism is not just about the person with whom you are sharing, because even if you refuse, God can make the rocks cry out. Evangelism is about experiencing God at work, in action, in love with people."

Now to Him who is able to do above and beyond all that we ask or think—according to the power that works in you—to Him be glory in the church and in Christ Jesus to all generations, forever and ever.

EPHESIANS 3:20–21

More tools FOR SHARING
YOUR FAITH *with others!*

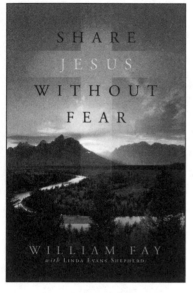

Share Jesus without Fear

Trade paper, $9.99, 192 pages
ISBN 0-8054-1839-3

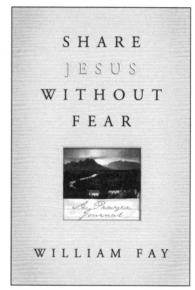

Share Jesus without Fear Journal

Trade paper, $9.99, 160 pages
ISBN 0-8054-4065-8

Also available:

Share Jesus without Fear Audio Book
$3.99, ISBN 0-8054-2298-6

Share Jesus without Fear New Testament, King James Version
$12.99, ISBN 1-55819-793-1

Share Jesus without Fear New Testament, Holman CSB®
$12.99, ISBN 1-58640-012-6

Share Jesus without Fear Student Edition
New Testament, Holman CSB®
$12.99, ISBN 1-58640-013-4